NORWAY

TIGER BOOKS INTERNATIONAL

Texts
Fabio Bourbon

Graphic design
Anna Galliani

Map
Giancarlo Gellona

The Publisher would like to thank the
Norwegian Tourism Board and in particular Elisabeth Ones

Contents

Urban Scenario, Human Scale..............................*page 30*
The Call of the Wide Open Spaces.......................*page 62*
The Sami, People of the Great North..................*page 94*
North of the Arctic Circle...................................*page 108*

1 *In the Lofoten Islands, north of the Arctic Circle, winter brings heavy snowfalls. When the thaw sets in and the sun shines again after the long Arctic night, this gleaming carpet of pristine whiteness offers a magical contrast with the bright colours of towns and villages along the coasts.*

2-3 *Hamnøy, on the island of Moskenesøya, is one of the many fishing villages sprinkled about the archipelago of the Lofotens.*

4-5 *Picturesque Nærøyfjord is a secondary branch of the immense Sognefjord which, with a length of 137 miles, is the longest fjord in the world. The fjords were formed from primordial glacial valleys which, "drowned" by the sea after the Earth's crust subsided, were transformed into deep inlets.*

6-7 *Ålesund, in the county of Møre og Romsdal, is one of Norway's most important fishing ports. It occupies a delightful position on the two islands of Ospøy and Nørvøy, separated only by a narrow channel. The town is renowned for the vibrant Art Nouveau architecture that characterizes most of its buildings.*

8 *Besides its medieval monuments and Hanseatic district, Bergen is famous for the distinctive bright colours of houses in the old part of the city. The most brightly painted of all are to be found on the peninsula jutting into the sea between the port and Puddenfjord.*

9 *From the towering granite cliff of Prekestolen there is a sheer drop into the incredibly blue waters of the Lysefjord. Situated only a few miles from Stavanger, this spectacular rock formation is the most famous vantage point in Scandinavia.*

12-13 *Through the centuries wars and fire have been the worse enemies of Norway's architectural heritage but Stavanger still boasts numerous old wooden buildings, overlooking its main streets.*

14-15 *The most northern regions of Norway are the undisputed realm of the Sami people, usually better known as Lapps. The traditional dwelling-place of their primarily nomadic populations is a cone-shaped tent, made from a frame of birchwood poles draped with reindeer skins.*

16-17 *This enchanting picture of a fjord was taken in the county of Sogn og Fjordane. The long Norwegian coastline - extending for no less than 13,000 miles, islands excluded - offers an incredible variety of landscapes and seascapes, from the deserted, rugged cliffs of the north to the gently undulating pasturelands of fjord country.*

18-19 *Prekestolen (Pulpit Rock) soars to a height of 2,000 feet. And viewed from above or - better still - from the waters of Lysefjord below, its perfectly square platform shape really does resemble a gigantic pulpit.*

This edition published in 1996 by TIGER BOOKS INTERNATIONAL PLC , 26a York Street Twickenham TW1 3LJ, England.

First published by Edizioni White Star. Title of the original edition: Norvegia, la terra dei fiordi. © World copyright 1996 by Edizioni White Star, Via Candido Sassone 22/24, 13100 Vercelli, Italy.

ISBN 1-85501-820-9

Printed in Singapore by Tien Wah Press. Color separations by Graphic Service, Milano, Italy.

Vesterålen

Lofoten

BODØ

ATLANTIC OCEAN

Svartisen ▲

Røssvatn

Børgefjell ▲

Frøya
Hitra

Trondheimsfjorden

TRONDHEIM ●

Trollheimen ▲

Dovrefjell

Jostedalsbreen

Jotunheimen

RØROS

Sognefjorden

Glitterind ▲

Gudbrandsdalen

BERGEN ●

Hardangerjøkulen

LILLEHAMMER ●

Hardangerfjorden

Mjøsa

Hardangervidda

Boknafjorden

OSLO ●

Glomma

STAVANGER ●

NORTH SEA

Oslofjorden

KRISTIANSAND ●

Skagerrak

Introduction

Every aspect of Norwegian life is influenced by two fundamental elements: sea and mountains, their ubiquitous presence made all the more forceful by their awe-inspiring dimensions. Norway is a country where man is and feels very small beside the imposing, primordial works of Nature, here barely touched by signs of civilization. Scenes of rare harmony and beauty are offered by never-ending expanses of green forest, dazzling white snow melting into constant trickles of water, deep blue fjords and rugged grey mountains. The sounds heard here are loud and yet mysterious, the bracing air is pungent with the fragrance of woods and ocean, the light is constantly changing. A few clouds, a storm and the atmosphere is transformed: gentle meadows reflected only minutes before in crystal-clear waters suddenly look dark and threatening. But the clouds soon roll away and the soft green of the grass returns.

Majesty and variety are the common denominators of Norwegian panoramas: a scene may be dominated by sheer mountain cliffs or gentle hills; one branch of a fjord may be bordered by apple orchards in blossom, another fringed by towering walls of rock, populated only by seagulls. Every landscape conveys a sense of awe. Holding the entire nation in thrall is the sea, its waters lapping over 995 miles of coastline. With its fjords, the sea forces its way deep into the heart of the country, it encompasses myriads of islands and skerries, its waters break in furious waves against jutting headlands or caress beaches with the warming currents of the Gulf Stream. Beyond North Cape, the sea turns to solid ice, clutching the Svalbard islands in its frozen grip. Right down its length, in both the north and south, the Norwegian seaboard is a succession of jagged inlets and arms which scissor their way far into glacial valleys. Whether enclosed by soaring rock cliffs or spread out in a maze of islets, the fjords are the very image of Norway's charm, hallmark of a land on the far edge of the world, a place of lyrical beauty. Although a constant presence, the sea is revealed in a new light in thousands of unforgettable scenarios: from the port of Oslo to Svartisen glacier, from Narvik, iron ore capital, to the peninsula of Varanger, tinged with red by the midnight sun.

In terms of natural splendour, the stunning seascapes of Norway are rivalled only by its mountains, with their bare rock faces or flanks

green with pine forests. They form the huge bone structure of the country, dividing Norway from Sweden. The land of the Vikings has little flat terrain and fertile soil: hills and mountains occupy practically every region, relaxing their grip only in the far north, where their place is taken by the frozen wastes of the tundra.

But Norway is not only sea and mountains: it abounds with forests, rushing torrents, lakes and ice-caps and these are the substance of its art and literature. Its fascinating legends - populated by mountain-dwelling giants of stone - were inspired by the rugged physical features of the coastline, which sometimes personified the forces of evil, sometimes the forces of good. Little has changed since the days - long, long ago - when the old man of Vage fell in love with a beautiful girl of Leka; he travelled south and, caught by the light of the sun, was turned into stone, along with all his people. Nature - untamed but bountiful - is always the protagonist: in stories about cod-fishing in the freezing-cold waters of the Lofotens; in the music of Grieg who, from his Bergen home, described with swift phrases the harmony of the fjords; in the writings of Ibsen and in the early paintings of Munch; in adventures related by friends over a cup of coffee in a little house in Trondheim.

The natural environment is bound to condition life in a country like Norway: only a very small part of its territory - no more than 4% - can be considered inhabited, and no other nation in continental Europe has a lower population density. Once great explorers and conquerors, the Norwegians of today have little in common with the stereotyped image of Scandinavians: far from being reserved and introverted, they are friendly, open people, with a willingness to help that on occasion leaves people on the receiving end of their kindness lost for words. In few other countries in the world could a traveller arrive at an attractive little railway station in some remote village, convinced he has just missed the last train of the day, only to be amazed at the immediate reaction of a lovely-looking station "mistress": a quick phone call to the driver and the train - rather than leave a customer stranded - returns to pick him up. In reverse! Even more amazing, the passengers greet the newcomer not with frowns and complaints, but with amused expressions and words of encouragement. Still on the subject of trains, where else but in Norway could you book a seat by phone, leaving your first name only, and be greeted a few days later by a smiling clerk, with your ticket ready to be paid and collected? Honesty and trust are qualities every Norwegian appears to be born with.

In this magical land where the human scale of things prevails, you may even see a staid gentleman unhurriedly cutting the grass growing on the roof of his house (a turf roof is in fact an effective way to help reduce heat loss). Confronted with scenes like this, visitors experience a feeling of respect mixed with envy. The Norwegians lead the world in their responsiveness to the innovative offerings of the modern age and yet their existence is evidence of an entrenched natural life force that reasserts and exalts their origins. These men and women with straw-coloured hair and deep-set eyes have learnt how to enjoy the conquests of civilized society while showing their respect for and intimacy with nature; they have transformed a cult-like love of physical exercise in the "great outdoors" into an expression of inner strength and vitality.

As a celebrated architect, Sverre Fehn, pointed out, no-one plants trees in Norway because there are already so many, nature having been left undisturbed. Norwegians like Nature the way they live it, shrouded in mists and low-lying clouds: perhaps this is why, beneath their apparent Nordic aloofness, they are more romantic than people imagine. It is not hard to find occasions to put them to the test. If you search beneath the slightly rough and often seemingly unfriendly surface of a character shaped by the rigorous climate of this land, you will make some amazing encounters, far more effective than words at describing the essence of the Norwegian people. Hospitality, a deep-rooted sense of national identity and enthusiastic awareness of their country's beauty, are revealed not by what they say, but by the way in which they lead their everyday lives.

This does much to explain the life-style chosen by someone like Roy Sandvik.
This outgoing, friendly man is a telephone engineer working on line maintenance in Longyearbyen, the tiny main town of the Svalbard islands, a remote outpost of human life situated at a latitude of 78 degrees north, in the midst of the freezing Arctic Ocean. Carried away by his own enthusiasm, he assured us that nothing could keep him away for long from this magical world wrapped in thick mists and gripped by eternal ice. What many other people would consider a hostile and desolate wasteland is, to his eyes, an enchanted world, an amazing

20 *The splendid cathedral of Trondheim is the most important monument of medieval origin in Scandinavia. Founded towards the end of the 11th century by King Olav III, it suffered destruction and fire and has been restructured several times. While the transept and chapter-house are in Norman Romanesque style, the rest of the building is Gothic; the highly ornate façade was completed only recently.*

21 top *Tromsø now has a population of 55,000, many more than in the 1930s when it became known as the Gateway to the Arctic: it was - in effect - the point of departure for the expeditions to the North Pole made by Roald Amundsen and Umberto Nobile. As present-day claims to fame, the town has the world's most northerly university and brewery.*

21 bottom *Most Norwegian buildings were once made of wood, the construction material easiest to procure and use. However, this fact put towns at enormous risk since devastating fires occurred all too frequently. This explains why the picturesque mining village of Røros, which has survived intact right up to the present day, is such an exception.*

22-23 *Besides being Norway's capital, seat of government and residence of its monarchy, Oslo is the country's most densely populated city, with over half a million inhabitants. It stands in a magnificent position at the head of the long and ragged Oslofjord, which is ice-free all year round. Its busy tourist port is dominated by the twin towers of the City Hall, built between 1933 and 1950, now the city's best known landmark.*

microcosm with new secrets to reveal each day. And thanks to his fervour, we too were better able to appreciate its wonderland qualities. It is impossible to conceal the truth about the rigours of the climate and the short-lived summers, not long enough even to soften memories of the terrible winter. And yet the spectacular beauty of the midnight sun which shines day and night from April 19 to August 23, the battle cry of the quarrelsome arctic tern, and the magical sight of drifting icebergs can far more effectively play on emotions than anything the imagination can offer.

Likewise, had we not met Roar Justad, we might never have become so deeply attached to the Lofoten Islands, situated some 124 miles north of the Arctic Circle. These islands - undisputed realm of wind and sea birds - are bathed in a fragile, unreal light. Dominated by high mountains whose steep cliffs rise up from the cold waters of the Vestfjord, their scenery is straight out of a Nordic saga. Beneath his grumpy bear exterior this man conceals a heart of gold. Over twenty years ago he turned his old fisherman's cottage in Stamsund into a youth hostel where he has since welcomed travellers from every corner of the globe. He has stories to tell to each and every one of them and for many he has become a living legend; a considerable number have returned to visit him years later, sometimes taking their own children with them. He was the person who taught us the basics about manoeuvring a rowing boat and explained the mysteries of the Northern Lights. He also told us the way to the village of Unstad and the white-sand beach of Utakleiv, two of the least known and most fascinating places on the island, where on stormy days the wind battles with the waves, seizes them, shapes them into columns of froth and then decapitates them, crushing the foam into a powdery wetness. Most important of all, he made it possible for us to "feel" the beauty of his world: a world of huge rocks tossed into the sea to form a wall of titanic proportions, almost vertical granite cliffs like the ramparts of a fortress, shores scattered with rocks smoothed into outlandish shapes, tiny bays to which "rorbuer" - the red-painted cottages typical of the region - cling like oysters.

As we stood on a headland and looked down at Roar's house, extending on piles over the waters of the harbour, we realized that - in this land where the master plan has already been imposed by fjords, rivers and mountains - the built environment contributed by man is in perfect harmony with the creations of Nature. The charm of these houses lies in their simple, rational proportions, while their vibrant colours - red, yellow and green - convey a sense of strength and vitality in surprising contrast to the soft light characteristic of the north. These utterly basic lines and colours help us understand the complex equilibrium that exists here, between man and the world around him. Norwegian homes are the practical expression of the very idea of habitation, functional yet elegant in both their exterior and interior design. In the little towns and villages huddled along the winding arms of the sea in Fjordland or on the coasts of the Vesterålen islands, homes are equally warm and inviting and they reflect the same quiet taste.

Not even the cities of Oslo, Bergen, Stavanger or Trondheim can detract from the flawless grace of snow-covered valleys, mountain ranges and labyrinthine coasts since the formation of the territory always sets the rules. Fjords and forests do not only mark Norway's boundaries, they also determine its people's way of life. And despite the austere climate, life in Norway is vibrant and dynamic, focused firmly on the future while still clinging to the sagas of the distant past. Hardly surprising: as soon as the last houses of any city or town are left behind, the vast expanse of the horizon or the looming presence of massed spruce trees instil a sense of subjection and awe. In the half-light you become aware - or so you think - of mysterious, almost imperceptible movements. Your apprehension makes the very air seem harder to breathe, as though some terrible secret were about to be revealed. Man feels very small when confronted with breathtaking evidence of primordial forces, like the rocky cliff of Trollveggen or the boundless moors of the Hardangervidda plateau.

Small wonder that still today - as in the remote past when the glaciers melted and made way for forests - strange things can occur during long Norwegian nights: out from caverns, nooks and crannies, from beneath the gnarled roots of centuries-old trees come the trolls, mythical beings with eight teeth and eight fingers, some big, some small but, irrespective of size, determined to have fun playing pranks on unsuspecting victims (although they are apparently not without a streak of kindness too). Trolls are seen just about everywhere in Norway, usually at the doorway to souvenir shops. These funny little creatures with big noses have irresistible tourist appeal, but their ubiquitous presence also says a lot about Norwegians' attachment to legends and to certain of their untouchable traditions.

Sure enough, if you take a good look around a Norwegian home, you practically always find a troll in some shape or form tucked away in a corner, maybe on a window-sill, together with assorted pieces of pottery and ornaments, beautifully worked wreaths of dried flowers, exquisite needlework and tiny, coloured candles. To passers-by their decorative effect conveys an impression of warmth and hospitality, conjuring up thoughts of happy, bygone days, a bit like the fragrance of home-baked apple pie, straight from the oven. In Scandinavia windows have no shutters - almost as though to let in more light - and the thoroughly Nordic custom of decorating them has in some places become practically an artform: a walk through the narrow streets of Røros, an old mining village in the Trøndelag region, is rather like visiting an outdoor museum in which each painting is in fact a window.

In Norway reality and fable combine to create a world that offers the best of both. They are different yet complementary faces of a country which has retained the human scale of its distant past, but is also justifiably proud of its achievements in the age of technology.

The backbone of modern Norwegian society is its constitutional monarchy, with an approach to government strongly influenced by the needs of both population and environment. Land use planning is attributed great importance: a key objective is to make certain services typically found in cities available throughout the country and thus stop migration from rural areas, while protecting and conserving the natural environment.

The Norwegians have seen the errors of past ways: at one time people believed nature could stand up to man's wilful tampering without a protest but they eventually recognized that the rush to modernize had its negative side. Now they have instead built power stations inside mountains or tunnelled beneath the sea so as to keep the impact on the landscape to a minimum.

The results of this commitment and concern are instantly evident in Oslo, one of the few capitals of the world where you can still pick mushrooms in city parks, swim in the waters of the port or go walking in forests which seem to be pushing their way into the suburbs. And yet Oslo also has a lively cultural life, with many monuments and museums as well as amenities for diversion and leisure. Oslo stands at the head of Oslofjord, overlooking a wide bay and separated from the open sea by a myriad of tongues of land and tree-covered islets stretching as far as the eye can see. The city covers 174 square miles, possibly a larger area than any other capital; and yet it has only half a million inhabitants, corresponding to 13 per cent of Norway's entire population. Three quarters of Oslo's metropolitan area is occupied by green spaces and lakes, many of them situated in the vast suburbs where the quality of life can be exceptionally good - a far cry from the urban sprawl and concrete jungles typical of big cities elsewhere in Europe. Only in the centre - near the Royal Palace or the gaunt twin towers of the City Hall, or along Karl Johans Gate, the main and busiest thoroughfare - does Oslo convey the hectic pace and lively image typical of modern cities; but even here the noise of traffic is relieved by the more melodious sounds of flutes, guitars and even harps played by omnipresent street musicians. Even in the midst of this hustle and bustle of people, sounds and colours, there is evidence of another distinctive aspect of the spirit of Oslo: the universal Norwegian passion for wide open spaces. Very close at hand, for instance, is the peace and tranquillity of Vigeland Park: here over two hundred statues of human figures - frozen in the act of running, leaping, playing, embracing - depict episodes in the cycle of life, from childhood to old age. The ultra-modern architecture of Aker Brygge - the spectactular new shopping centre built by the harbour, where nothing but grey wharves stood until a few years ago - symbolizes a city projected towards the future. But the endless hills and countless islands all around present a totally different side of Oslo, a city where old customs die hard and a feeling of the past lingers in the air.

If you roam around the numerous small islands of Oslofjord, you find in each tiny inlet an isolated house, with its jetty, moored boat and wisp of smoke rising up from a barbecue. It is as though the city has disappeared, hidden from view by birches and willows. Irrespective of age and class, Oslonians share a passionate love - verging on addiction - for the Marka, the vast metropolitan forest area which extends around the city. Criss-crossing the woods are hundreds of miles of paths, ideal for excursions when the weather is fine and for cross-country skiing in winter. The Marka is not considered simply the green heart of the capital, as it might be elsewhere: it is the "other Oslo", which makes life livable in the part made of concrete and stone.

Once you have understood the spirit of Oslo,

24-25 *Cheerfully-painted wooden houses nestling together along the narrow streets of old Bergen testify to the Norwegian people's embedded love of tradition. A perfect synthesis of ancient and modern worlds, this splendid city is the ideal place to really get to know and appreciate the Nordic spirit.*

26-27 The Lofotens are separated from one another by narrow channels renowned for their extremely powerful currents (the Maelstrom made famous by Jules Verne in "Twenty Thousand Leagues under the Sea", for it was here that Captain Nemo's Nautilus was swallowed up by the seething waters). And yet these islands appear to form a single chain of mountains descending to the sea on the distant horizon. This is why the archipelago is also called the Lofoten "Wall".

28-29 Norway is a land of vast open spaces. The country has a population of around 4.5 million but its people occupy only 4 per cent of a territory covering 125,000 square miles.

you have understood Norway and the Norwegians: people who are informal in their style of dress and behaviour, but who show an exceptionally sane and civilized attitude towards the fundamental things in life. This does not mean Norway and its population are totally without faults: admiration for the Norwegians' general concern for preserving nature in the raw is sometimes deflated by evidence of horrors which leave foreign observers speechless, for instance, the recent decision to allow the resumption of whale and seal hunting. Its proponents maintain that the north of Norway has been especially hard-hit by the effects of the recession and, particularly, by the decline of the cod-fishing industry. They even blame the seals for serious damage caused to fishing nets, which they get caught in during spring when migrating towards the Svalbard islands. There's no denying that putting whalers back into service or slaughtering seal pups for their valuable skins may be an effective way of helping solve the country's serious unemployment problems. It is nevertheless amazing that a nation which leads the world in other respects cannot come up with some less controversial solutions.

In recent years the Laplanders who live in the far north have also seen their way of life revolutionized. But the collapse of traditional activities - like reindeer-herding, seriously hit by the Chernobyl disaster - has led them to discover that tourism can be turned into a real gold mine, with a relatively contained impact on the environment. In places like Kautokeino, Alta and Tromsø you can now buy - though not cheaply - beautiful objects made from reindeer horn, birchwood ladles, exquisitely crafted silver tankards and adornments made from finest-quality metals, until a few years ago used only to embellish traditional costumes worn on ceremonial occasions. It is a flourishing business, swelled each year by the many thousands of foreign visitors drawn here by their fascination with the Arctic and their desire to see North Cape, northernmost point of the continent of Europe. The great majority of the Sami - as the approximately 60,000 members of this legendary ethnic minority prefer to be called - have abandoned their former nomadic existence. They are now trying to adapt to social and economic change while safeguarding their traditions and cultural values, which they intend to preserve at all costs. Their line of conduct is to be considered exemplary, especially now that Norway has become an extremely popular tourist destination.

More and more people are coming here in search of wide open spaces, boundless horizons, virgin lakes and forests, elsewhere in short supply or gone forever. From 1977 to 1988 the Sami people fought bitterly - and successfully - to stop the construction of a dam on the River Altaelva, in order to save several villages and a vast area of tundra from disappearing beneath the waters of its reservoir. Supporters of progress at all costs may have been infuriated by their determined opposition, but the outcome was a victory for common sense and longsightedness. Protecting and conserving the natural beauty of one's homeland is a long-term investment, with rewards far greater than the easy-come-by earnings of a short-term vision, indifferent to the distant future.

Lovers of climbing and trekking, birdwatching and winter sports are discovering the delights of Norway in increasing numbers. And so are visitors for whom tourism means essentially relaxation, but with the added bonus of an unspoiled natural setting. Where else could one explore a place like Finse, on the Hardangervidda plateau, where a breathtaking landscape of glaciers, lakes and tundra extends as far as the eye can see? And yet these few houses, seemingly in "the middle of nowhere", at an altitude of over 4000 feet, are actually on a train line with a regular service that takes only a couple of hours to reach Bergen, one of Norway's liveliest and most densely populated cities. Here, instead, a few minutes' walk is sufficient to leave the civilized world behind you. Wearing a rucksack on your back and a pair of good boots, you can tramp for as long as a week without encountering any sign of human life. During the day you may come across a timid, sharp-muzzled fox or a group of swift-moving hares; amongst the bushes you may spot a willow ptarmigan or, between the branches of a birchtree, the watchful eyes of a snow owl. At night, squatted around a camp fire, you wait patiently for the lemmings: curious by nature and always hungry, these funny little rodents never fail to appear. The same can happen on the mountains of Telemark, in the valleys of Sognefjord or when surrounded by the immense tundra of Finnmark, habitat of reindeer and majestic elk. Scattered about this realm of mosses and lichens, far from the region's few towns and villages, are isolated refuge huts in which travellers can spend the night. And when the midnight sun splashes the heavens with breathtaking colours, they scan the horizon in wonder, listening to the soft and gently monotonous song of the wind.

Civilization, traffic, the tedious rituals of everyday life seem remote, alien, unimaginable. To preserve this uncontaminated environment is no mean task. From one day to the next the concrete and asphalt, trucks, cars and high-tension pylons which have a stranglehold on much of the "civilized" world could start to encroach on this world too. Fortunately - as we were told some years ago by Liv, a pretty young student from Bergen - Norway's younger generation is increasingly aware of these issues and intends to continue in the present, positive direction: they know full well that the country's growth must go hand-in-hand with respect for the natural environment and attachment to traditions which are part and parcel of its culture. Norway - said Liv - is a relatively young nation, officially in existence only since 1905, when the union with Sweden was dissolved. It has a vast territory, huge distances and a tiny population.

As was only to be expected, the prosperity that followed discovery of oil in the North Sea in the '70s was enthuasistically welcomed by one and all, and the country rushed to modernize. Tens of formerly isolated villages could at last be reached along tarmaced roads; tunnels were dug, bridges, dams and power stations built. Only later, when the euphoria had faded, did people realize they had been wrong to trust blindly in nature's ability to recover from the wounds inflicted by "progress". Growing sectors of the population accepted that the price to pay in years to come for upsetting the ecological equilibrium was too high.

The government therefore began to introduce far-reaching measures to protect the environment. A strong sense of national identity - but with none of the negative aspects - has done the rest. The superb organization of the Winter Olympic Games in Lillehammer showed the world how a modern nation can successfully reconcile social and technological development with respect for nature and the environment. As an outpost of one of Europe's last remaining expanses of wilderness, Norway is engaged in a constant battle with problems caused by the unstoppable march of "progress", but it appears to be winning. Its mission is undeniably a challenging one: to pass on intact to future generations a natural heritage that includes the cliffs of Værøy with their immense population of sea birds, the splendid fjord of Geiranger, the eternal glaciers of Folgefonn and the rocky massif of Dovrefjell. It is a tremendous task but one that will reap immeasurable rewards.

Urban Scenario, Human Scale

30 top *Oslo is the oldest capital city of Scandinavia. Founded by King Harald Hårdråde in the 11th century, for several hundred years it remained a small village gathered around its cathedral church. Around 1300 King Håkon V "promoted" Oslo to capital status and began building the Akershus fortress, which still dominates the port today: it now looks much as it did after reconstruction in the 17th century by Christian IV.*

30 bottom *In the last 25 years or so Oslo has experienced a building boom. Ultra-modern buildings are now a feature of the cityscape, particularly in the harbour area and around the railway station.*

31 *Grensen is one of the city's main thoroughfares. This wide boulevard - its pavements lined with shops, chic boutiques and fashionable cafés and restaurants - leads from the Domkirke (Cathedral) up to Slottsparken, the most prominent green space in central Oslo.*

32-33 *Oslo can always offer something of interest: pictured here is Aker Brygge, a bustling shopping mall and lively cultural centre built in recent years on the fjord waterfront, on a site previously occupied by sombre grey wharves.*

Oslo, stress-free metropolis

34 *Oslo is a busy cosmopolitan city, hub of domestic and international communications, Norway's major financial centre and home of an important university. In many respects it is the only true metropolis in Norway. And yet it retains the human scale of a small community: here the pace of life is far from frenetic and there is always time and space for momentary diversion, even right in the centre of town.*

35 top *Fronted by groups of statues and decorated with sculptures, murals and paintings specially commissioned from the country's best known artists, the City Hall is itself a kind of museum of contemporary Norwegian art.*

35 bottom *In 1921 Gustav Vigeland signed a contract with Oslo City Council which led to the creation of a sculpture park now universally recognized as one of the most unusual and exciting manifestations of contemporary art. There are 150 statues in the park: culminating with the celebrated Monoliten, 56 feet in height, the figures represent the different ages of man, from infancy to old age, and the moods and emotions associated with each.*

36-37 *Standing at the far end of Karl Johans Gate, one of the city's main arteries, is the imposing neoclassical Royal Palace; the magnificent park surrounding it is open to the public, and it is one of the most popular spots of greenery in Oslo.*

37 top *Although Frogner Park is best known for Gustav Vigeland's statues, the Oslo Bymuseum is also located here, housed in a late 18th-century palace: its interiors with authentic furnishings recreate the atmosphere of the Romantic period.*

37 centre *Oslo's most important religious building is the Domkirke, the Evangelical cathedral constructed at the end of the 17th century, extensively rebuilt in the 1800s and restored after World War Two.*

37 bottom *Perhaps the most famous museum in Oslo is the Vikingskipene, with its three authentic Viking longships. Best preserved is the Oseberg ship, with its ornate carvings; it was used as the tomb of a queen, discovered together with the precious objects buried with her.*

Bergen,
pearl of the fjords

38-39 *Bergen - Norway's second city and main North Sea port - is situated in a scenic position at the head of Byfjord and encircled by hills. Established in the 11th century, it boasts many historic monuments and has a vibrant cultural life.*

39 top *At the far end of the port is Torget, the square where a daily market - of a different kind - is held: besides the usual souvenirs, flowers and fruit, there are stalls with glistening heaps of freshly caught fish, just unloaded from North Sea fishing boats. Sandwiches stuffed with smoked salmon and crabmeat, for instance, eaten here on the spot, are an experience not to be missed.*

40 In spite of numerous fires and other disasters, Bergen still has many exceptional testimonies of its past. One of the city's main historic sites is Mariakirken (St.Mary's Church), dating from the 12th-century and built in Norman Romanesque style. Its austere façade, enclosed between two massive towers, is embellished by a splendid doorway; the interior - with its almost cloistered atmosphere - boasts a magnificent 16th-century pulpit and rich baroque furnishings.

41 top Founded in 1070 by the Viking king Olav Kyrre, Bergen experienced notable growth in the Middle Ages, eventually becoming capital of Norway and main port of Scandinavia. A splendid legacy of the city's glorious past is the fortress of Bergenhus, built in the 11/12th centuries. One of the buildings within its walls is the Gothic Håkonshallen, a Great Hall used for ceremonies.

41 bottom Rosenkrantztarnet is also part of the Bergenhus complex. These fortifications were enlarged and embellished in the 16th century by the governor after whom they were named. The entire fortress suffered serious damage in World War Two but, thanks to years of careful restoration work, its buildings have regained their original splendour.

42-43 *Many people consider Bergen to be Norway's loveliest city and this opinion is doubtless shared by most of the foreign visitors who, in summer especially, make it a very popular destination. The houses pictured here are in Bryggen, the old district established from 1500 onwards by German traders of the Hanseatic League.*

Ålesund and Tromsø, towns of the sea

44-45 *The church of Ålesund was rebuilt in 1909 in neo-Norman style; its interior, illuminated by stunning Art Nouveau stained-glass windows, was entirely frescoed by Enevold Thomt between 1918 and 1928.*
In 1988 the town was awarded the important Houen national prize for the efforts made by the city's authorities and population to preserve its outstanding architectural heritage. Ålesund is the only town in the world to reflect, in every respect, the spirit of Art Nouveau.

46-47 *Overlooking the channel port of Ålesund are a number of attractive buildings, formerly used as warehouses and fish-processing factories; now restored and totally refurbished, they have been turned into upmarket homes, smart offices for successful businesses and expensive restaurants.*

48-49 *Seat of Troms county and long-established as an urban settlement (its origins date back to the mid-13th century), Tromsø is one of the most important towns in Arctic Norway. Built on a small island, it was permanently linked to the mainland only in 1960 by a spectacular 3400-feet bridge. Situated in a suburban area on the mainland (in the foreground of this photo) is the modern Tromsdal Church, which has one of the world's largest stained-glass windows.*

Stavanger,
a "new town" built by oil

50-51 *Stavanger is a major international port and Norway's fourth city in terms of population. It is also one of the country's most important industrial centres, and the chief town and seat of local government in Rogaland county. Although it has developed considerably over the last few decades, Stavanger still looks much as it did in bygone days and its architectural heritage remains intact.*

52-53 *Stavanger's finest monument, the Domkirke (Cathedral), was built in Norman Romanesque style from 1125 but partially rebuilt along Gothic lines after the great fire of 1272. The flat apse, enclosed by two towers, has a splendid mullioned window set off by four statues. Inside is a grandiose baroque pulpit, dated 1658.*

Røros,
mining community of the past

54-55 *The old mining village of Røros is in Sor-Trøndelag county, at the very heart of east/central Norway. The older part of the town, dominated by the stone church dedicated in 1784, is comprised of clusters of picturesque wooden houses built by miners from the mid-17th century onwards.*

55 *With its unique townscape - its houses often have turf roofs to make them more resistant to the rigours of winter - the entire older part of Røros has been made a national monument. It is now a much-visited outdoor museum where numerous cultural events of international importance take place, especially in summer.*

Trondheim,
ancient heart of the nation

57 top right *Perched on a hill 230 feet above Trondheim is Kristiansten Fort, which affords a fine view over the city. It was built by French architect Jean Caspar de Cicignon after a terrible fire destroyed much of the town in 1681.*

57 bottom right *Since the earliest days of Trondheim, the mouth of the river Nidelva has been a busy channel port; one of the city's bridges is the Bybrua, an attractive drawbridge built in the 1800s.*

58-59 *Built over the grave of Olav Haraldson - Norway's patron saint and the king who converted Norwegians to Christianity - the magnificent cathedral of Trondheim is one of the country's most historically significant buildings. A major contribution to this architectural gem in green-grey soapstone was made by English master-builders and it is to them that its resemblance to Lincoln cathedral is attributed; the statues ornating its splendid façade portray biblical figures, saints and monarchs.*

Narvik, on the road to North Cape

60 top *The town of Narvik, in Norway's Arctic region, has great economic importance. From its port sail ships carrying iron ore from the mines of Kiruna, in Swedish Lapland. The railway line connecting the two towns, completed in 1902, is the only one in the world situated entirely above the Artic Circle.*

60 bottom *In World War Two Narvik became an important strategic target; it was occupied several times by Germans and then by the Allies and suffered extensive devastation.*
Almost entirely rebuilt in the post-war period, it is now a busy and lively place, a summer staging post for tourists heading for North Cape.

60-61 *The lookout point at the top of Fagernes (4170 feet high) can be reached by cable car and affords a fine view over Narvik and the Ofotfjord. It is also an ideal spot, at any time of day, to observe the "midnight sun" which shines here from the end of May to mid-July.*

The Call of the Wide Open Spaces

62 top *Norway is the least populated country in Europe after Iceland but there seem to be tiny villages almost everywhere, especially along the coast. In effect, less than a quarter of the population are city-dwellers. Pictured here is a small fishing village on the island of Magerøya, in the Lofotens.*

62 bottom *In the Lofoten Islands mountain ridges and cliffs entwine as they drop down to the dark, threatening waters of the ocean, since time immemorial the only source of livelihood for the small fishing communities along these shores. For anyone not born here the idea of spending the severe Arctic winter in such a place is practically inconceivable.*

63 *Geirangerfjord is one of the most beautiful in Norway. It winds its way between sheer, narrow cliffs down which come great waterfalls with poetic names - the Seven Sisters (in the photo), Suitor and Bridal Veil - all of them originating from local legends and sagas.*

64-65 *From Flåm, a pretty hamlet at the head of Aurlandsfjord, a mountain railway with the steepest gradient in the world climbs up to Myrdal, on the main Oslo-Bergen line. For the passengers travelling high up along practically vertical cliffs it is a spectacular and thrilling ride.*

65 *The Flåm-Myrdal line has been described as one of the most daring engineering achievements of the 20th century and the Norwegians are justly proud of it. During the summer months, just before reaching Myrdal the train stops for a few minutes solely to let tourists take a good look at a breathtaking waterfall which comes plunging down only feet from the railway line.*

66-67 *From high up above Stalheim Gorge there is a wonderful view over the valley of Nærøy and its celebrated fjord. A ferry service connects Flåm, a well-known tourist resort, with Gudvangen. Here a tiny road with twenty or more hairpin bends zigzags up the mountain-side: a hair-raising ride....*

Land of fjords

68-69 *Cruising down the Nærøy fjord - the narrowest in Norway and certainly one of the loveliest - can be a truly poetic experience. Set deep between rugged mountains of unspoiled* *scenic beauty, this arm of water winds its way further and further inland, occasionally passing a tiny village whose few inhabitants seem oblivious of their remoteness from the rest of the world.*

The ice giant

70-71 *In Lower Central Norway, icy tongues from the immense icefields of the Jostedal glacier - the largest in continental Europe - descend along narrow valleys carved by primordial glaciers. This lake has formed in the morainic ravine left by the glacier over the last 200 years; during this time it has retreated more than 3 miles.*

Living at
minus 40

72 left *From the 1960s onwards, as the shoals of cod got smaller and catches continued to shrink, the immigration which populated the Lofotens during the last century became no more than a sad memory. All that now remains of those heroic days are hundreds of red cottages scattered along the coast: these simple wooden cabins are "rorbuer", once the homes of seasonal fishermen, now rented to summer visitors.*

72-73 *Bright red was the colour typically used to paint the "rorbuer" as well as most farmhouses and other rural buildings, the*

reason being that red paint was the cheapest. People who could afford to spend more used yellow, while the wealthy painted their houses white, the most costly and least hard-wearing colour of all.

74-75 *Northwards from Tromsø the immensity of the landscape gives it an increasingly unreal, almost alien look. The few houses clustered along the shores face south, to make the most of the sun's light and warmth, a rare and precious commodity 250 miles above the Arctic Circle.*

76-77 *Finnmark, Norway's most northerly county, is larger than the whole of Denmark and yet has only 80,000 inhabitants. This is the realm of boundless horizons and solitude, Europe's last frontier of nature in the raw. Pictured here is a stretch of the splendid Kvænangen fjord, as it suddenly appears to visitors motoring along the E6, the road which leads to North Cape.*

78 Occupying the northernmost part of Norway is Finnmark, where the Arctic tundra dominates the landscape and only in the most sheltered areas are there occasional pockets of green, mostly birch and dwarf willow trees. During the thaw melting snow turns rivers into rushing torrents: impossible as it may seem, summer is just around the corner.

79 *The scenery of Finnmark - this photo was taken near Karasjok - is consistently awe-inspiring, ideal for people who adore wide open spaces and solitude.*

Norwegians love the tranquillity of their vast country and often retreat to "hytter", isolated wood cabins deep in the heart of a forest, like the one shown here.

80-81 *The lofty vantage point of Flydalsjuvet affords a breathtaking view of the village of Geiranger and the Geirangerfjord, so beautiful it is now regularly included in the tourist itineraries of cruise ships and boat trips.*

81 right *The area surrounding Åndelsnes, at the head of the Romsdalfjord, is famous for its permanently snowcapped mountains. Their peaks attract climbers of every nationality, challenged by some of the highest, practically vertical rock faces in the world.*

82-83 *The ten dizzying bends of Trollstigen ("trolls' causeway"), hewn out of solid rock, are perhaps the most thrilling part of the Golden Route, which links Åndelsnes with the Geirangerfjord. Clinging to the wall of a glacial valley, it is one of the steepest main roads in Europe.*

84-85 *Much of Norway is covered by lakes, forests and mountains. But 3% of its land area is intensively farmed and for many food products the country is self-sufficient. There are more than 100,000 farms, often in isolated but stunningly beautiful places.*

86-87 *From Geiranger, the pretty village on the fjord of the same name, a steep road with twenty bends zigzags up to Djupvasshytta, at an altitude of 3400 feet. There is a lookout point here, on the shores of a lake which stays frozen until the beginning of summer. The mountain massif of Dalsnibba towers over this wild and beautiful area.*

88-89 *The Arctic summer is short but vigorously regenerative. The average temperature rarely creeps above 15 degrees C but the few flat areas are transformed into luxuriant green meadows which provide the hay needed to feed the herds through the long winter. Beyond the Arctic Circle trees are few and far between, even at lower altitudes; above 1300 feet only patchy lichen manages to survive.*

North Cape, at the far edge of Europe

90 *Whether your gaze falls on a huddle of brightly coloured cottages or on an inlet where the blue of the sea emulates the sky, the scenery on the island of Magerøya is consistently splendid. And yet, in their anxiety to reach Europe's highest latitude, many visitors fail to fully appreciate its stark beauty (though not the true nature lovers amongst them).*

90-91 *"There was silence above the land and only the gentle whisper of the wind and, now and then, the voice of a bird". The unadorned prose of Knut Hamsun - Nobel prizewinner for literature in 1920 - seems totally in tune with the majestic, silent landscapes of the island of Magerøya, known mainly as the place where the E6 highway comes to an end. North Cape is close at hand, but it can wait.*

92-93 *North Cape - situated on the island of Magerøya, at a latitude of 71 degrees 10' 21" north - is the northernmost point of the continent of Europe. This plateau high above the sea marks the extreme edge of a bare Arctic wasteland; in actual fact Knivskjellodden - a small peninsula visible on the horizon - is slightly further north but its far less panoramic position played against it when a decision was taken on where the European road network should come to an end.*

93 *North Cape is likely to disappoint a lot of people who come here expecting to have reached the "last frontier". The headland, on which stands a monument representing the Earth, is now everything but a wilderness - especially since an obtrusive-looking visitor centre was built here, selling mass-produced souvenirs and offering such amenities as a cinema with 220-degree screen. Too many tourists, too many cars, too much concrete: and yet along the seemingly never-ending road from Alta, the landscapes encountered have a spectacular and awesome beauty. For many people North Cape represents their "journey's end". Those who instead seek a more solitary brand of adventure can travel on, towards the peninsula of Varanger or even as far as Kirkenes, close to the border with Russia.*

The Sami, People of the Great North

94 *The Sami people live in tribes in the Arctic regions of Sweden, Finland and Russia, as well as Norway, and they are the real lords of the great empty spaces of the far north. Knowledge of their remotest origins is still based essentially on conjecture. They have always been nomads, dependent on reindeer which, until a few years ago, were their staple and their fortune. Now the Sami have their own representatives in parliament, their own radio stations, newspapers and magazines (the Sami language belongs to a totally different group from the other Scandinavian languages).*

95 *The traditional dress of Sami men is a heavy blue tunic richly finished with red bands and coloured ribbons, drawn in at the waist with a belt and worn over reindeer-leather trousers; the women's costume is longer and flared, with a fringed shawl to add a feminine touch. While all Sami have much the same footwear, their hats - and especially the ones worn by men - change in style from tribe totribe.*

96 Every year, around Easter, the Sami gather in the main towns of their region for festive celebrations and traditional races. Among the sporting events are racing with sleighs drawn by reindeer and lasso-throwing. There was a time when life was really hard for Laplanders: although things are now easier, their lifestyle is still conditioned by the severe polar climate and the vast size of the mostly desert-like terrain that is their home.

97 Today the Sami number about 35,000, three-fifths of them living under Norwegian administration. Easter is an important feast and every year tens of families gather in the town of Kautokeino to celebrate. Their festivities are now a famous spring event.

98-99 *One of the most spectacular tests of skill is sleigh-racing. All the competitions are open to both sexes, and Sami girls are particularly accomplished at lasso-throwing, a challenging feat. The Sami people do not like being referred to as Lapps: they consider it a derogatory term and have long fought to bring their old name back into use. Sami means "the people", and it recalls ancient times when these proud tribes were undisputed lords of an otherwise deserted world.*

100-101 *Once the races and contests are over, there is a church service attended by one and all. Originally followers of an animist religion, the Sami were mostly converted to Lutheran Christianity in the 17th century. But echoes of their ancestral beliefs are still evident, thanks mainly to young artists trying to rediscover their people's deeply embedded cultural roots.*

102-103 *Weddings are important occasions, when families have an opportunity to meet and also to continue old traditions. Ornate costumes are worn for the most important ceremonies and the girls - and not only the bride - parade in their finest jewellery made of exquisitely worked silver, mined in several places in Lapland.*

104 Herds of reindeer migrating in search of food always follow the same routes, which is why the Sami are continuously on the move. In spring the young animals are caught one by one and "branded". Each reindeer is held firmly by the horns while a small shape is cut in the lower part of its ear, to designate its owner.

105   *A Sami has just thrown a lasso and its noose, with amazing precision, will catch the horns of a reindeer. The comfortable lifestyle of Western society is a serious threat to the survival of Lapp traditions and many Sami have already opted for permanent homes in the towns of the north. Nevertheless a strong awareness of their cultural heritage is now developing, especially among young people who are keen to conserve the unique features of the ancient Sami ethos.*

106-107   *For everyday use skis and the traditional sleigh have been banished in favour of skidoos. Reindeer herding is hard work but still profitable, although the Chernobyl disaster made it necessary to put down thousands of animals. The Lapp economy is currently picking up, also as a result of government provisions aimed at helping reindeer herders and exploiting two important new resources: tourism and craft products.*

North of the Arctic Circle

108 top *Lying between latitude 68 and 69 degrees, the Lofoten Islands are a 119-mile-long archipelago which, in the north-east, closes the broad expanse of the Vestfjord. Besides the main islands - Rostlandet, Værøy, Moskenesøya, Flakstadøya, Vestvågøya and Austvågøya - it includes a myriad of small, uninhabited islands and skerries. Viewed from the mainland, the Lofotens look like a single mountain range rising up majestically from the sea. Dazzling light and clear air make colours even brighter and the red, yellow and green of the few houses stand out prominently against the snow-covered landscape. This picture of the Lofotens was taken inland, near Gravdal, in mid-April.*

108 bottom *Stamsund, with its line-up of red "rorbuer" along the old harbour, is one of the main towns on the island of Vestvågøya. This is a place where time seems to have stood still and life proceeds at a totally different pace.*

109 *Even in tiny inlets like Hamnøy bay fishing-boats can shelter from the fury of winter storms. Winds reaching over 75 miles an hour are not unusual in this part of the world and, at such times, the protection of the high surrounding cliffs can prove providential.*

110-111 *It may seem strange - considering how far north they lie - but the Lofotens are much more densely populated than Norway's interior and there are quite a few centres of population on the islands, like this group of houses near Laupstad.*

The Lofotens "wall"

112 *The loftiest mountains in the Lofotens rise 4000 feet but their shape makes them look much higher. The Lofotens have 25,000 inhabitants and 4,500 of them live in Svolvær (bottom), chief town of the archipelago.*

113 *A thick blanket of snow covers the Lofotens during the long winter months but, thanks to the Gulf Stream, the climate is less rigorous than might be expected. The temperature drops well below zero but can be as much as 15 or 20 degrees higher than in other places on the same latitude.*

114-115 Practically the entire Lofoten Islands are formed of granite-rock mountains cut almost perpendicular and shaped by glacial action during the Quaternary Period; geologists believe them to be among the oldest rock formations on Earth. Even in summer their peaks are covered by perennial snowfields.

116-117 The Lofotens have a richly indented coastline, with numerous coves, channels and sheltered bays, very wisely chosen as sites for villages, like this tiny community near Svolvær. The range of high mountains which forms the backbone of the archipelago acts as an effective barrier against the onslaught of winds and storms sweeping in from the open sea.

118-119 *Henningsvær, on the island of Austvågøya, is an important base of the Lofotens' fishing fleet. Fishing no longer produces the earnings it used to. Nevertheless, every year between January and March, hundreds of boats and thousands of fishermen gather here to catch the cod.*

119 *The exceptional abundance of fish in the waters around the Lofotens is due to the conformation of the ocean floor and to the strong currents which turn the Lofotfjord into a kind of unavoidable route for enormous shoals of cod and herring.*

120-121 *In the Lofoten Islands sea and mountains come together to create an awe-inspiring spectacle, made all the more impressive by the icy grip of winter. Face-to-face with these rock giants, covered in snow and lapped by the waters of the Vestfjord, visitors have the chilling sensation of having reached the very ends of the Earth.*

122 top *From a rocky outcrop behind the harbour of Stamsund, the vista sweeps across to the Lofotens Wall: a stunning sight even on stormy summer days, when the mountains are bathed in a constantly changing light as rain clouds chasing across the sky allow occasional glimpses of a dazzling sun.*

122 bottom *Nusfjord, a tiny huddle of "rorbuer" on the island of Flakstadøya, can be reached only by sea or along a bumpy dirt road several miles long. Its origins date back to the 16th century and it is one of the most authentic and picturesque villages of the Lofotens, now included on UNESCO's list of preservation-worthy sites.*

123 *Utakleiv is another of the delightful, out-of-this-world corners that still exist in the Lofotens. Situated on the island of Vestvagoya but facing the open sea, this picturesque huddle of houses is inhabited by just ten or so families. The only land access to the village is along an exceptionally scenic, winding dirt track, a journey that on stormy days requires a certain spirit of adventure.*

Svalbard, a "stone's throw" from the North Pole

124-125 *The archipelago of Svalbard straddles the 80th parallel and is 621 miles from the North Pole. In summer the tundra is brightened by multi-coloured flora.*

126-127 *Shown in this picture is part of the immense Nordenskjold glacier, facing the Russian settlement at Pyramiden.*

128 *Moored in Oslo harbour is a replica of a Viking longship: a testimonial to the Norsemen who once ruled this land.*

All pictures inside the book are by
Giulio Veggi / Archivio White Star
except the following:

Marcello Bertinetti / Archivio White Star:
pages 14-15, 102-103, 104-105,
106-107.

Fabio Bourbon:
pages 46-47, 122-123, 124-125,
126-127